Chakras

The Complete Chakra Guide, Including Chakra Healing, Chakra Meditation, Chakra Clearing and Much More!

Table of Contents

Introduction 1
Free Bonus 2
Chapter 1: What are Chakras? 3
Chapter 2: The Seven Chakras 5
Chapter 3: Opening and Chakra Clearing 16
Chapter 4: Signs of Imbalance in your Chakras 22
Chapter 5: Cleaning and Chakra Healing 27
Chapter 6: Chakra Meditation 32
Chapter 7: The History of Chakras 35
Chapter 8: Why Your Chakras May Be Imbalanced or Blocked 39
Chapter 9: Affirmations for Improving Your Chakras 43
Chapter 10: How Yoga Can Help Your Chakras 51
Chapter 11: How Crystals Can Help Your Chakras 55
Conclusion 59

Introduction

Thank you for taking the time to pick up this book on Chakras!

This book contains helpful information about chakras, how they work, and how they affect your life and health. This is also the recently updated 2nd edition of this book. It's been updated with a range of new information, and can now be considered a complete guide to chakras.

You will soon discover what the 7 chakras are, what they do, and how they affect you on a day to day basis. You will also learn about the history of chakras originates, and the theories behind the chakras.

Each chakra has the power to cause you physical and emotional harm if imbalanced or blocked. This guide will show you how to find which chakra is responsible for your particular illness, injury, or emotion.

Further, you will learn how to clear, balance, and heal your chakras so that positive energy is able to flow through them. This will result in you feeling more grounded, healthy, and full of energy.

This book will explain to you tips and techniques that will allow you to successfully keep your chakras in good health, through meditation, yoga, and among other activities.

With cleared and healthy chakras, you will be able to experience life at its best, and feel energetic and healthy all the time!

Thanks again for picking up this book, I hope you enjoy it!

Free Bonus

As a thank you for taking the time to download my book, I'd like to offer you a **FREE** bonus!

I have compiled a list of my '7 Keys For Successful Meditation', and have made it free for you to download.

You can CLICK HERE to claim your free copy, or click on the link below:
http://bit.ly/1F91lfl

Meditation helps you to clear and focus your mind, and allows you to gain better control over your thoughts and focus. Regular meditation can make it a lot easier to successfully engage in things like Reiki healing, aura viewing, and opening your third eye, as these all involve deep and powerful use of your mind and focus.

So download my free report today – CLICK HERE – and begin experiencing the amazing benefits of meditation today!

Chapter 1:
What are Chakras?

Chakra is a Sanskrit word, which literally translates to "wheel". People can also interpret it as "circle", "cycle" and "vortex". The term is commonly used in Yoga and Ayurveda, a system of Hindu tradition medicine, as well as meditation, and refers to the wheels of energy in the body. From the words meaning, chakras refer to the endless rotation of energy in the body. These are the energy centers that compose our entire system and consciousness.

The Purpose of Chakras

One can imagine a chakra as a pool from which water flows to and fro. All chakras are sources of energy. Each acts as a valve that regulates the flow of energy throughout the body system. It is not a physical thing, but rather an aspect of one's consciousness. An aura is one other example of an aspect of consciousness, and can be mildly compared to a chakra. Chakras, however, are denser enough in nature that one can feel their effect on daily living. Unlike auras, which people consider as an electromagnetic field surrounding the body, a chakra is found within the body and governs certain areas.

Chakras are positive influences on a person's wellbeing, when they are open, clean and balanced. Each chakra governs one area of a person's body, serving certain nerves and major organs along with associated emotional and psychological states of being. There are seven main chakras in a person's body. It is essential that they are not only open, but also maintained for overall wellness to ensure better physical health, and mental and emotional wellbeing.

History

The idea of chakras comes from an ancient tradition that started sometime between 1,000 and 500 B.C. It was first mentioned in the Vedas, India's oldest written tradition. The term literally meant a "wheel", and was originally called Cakravartins. They referred to the rulers' chariot wheels, and a metaphorical reference to the sun, which was described as having a *triumphant chariot that traverses the world*.

It has been used, referred to and recognized in yoga, meditation and the Ayurvedic system. It was not until the 8th century when the hierarchies of chakras became well known. Over the years, chakras were recognized as the bridge to enlightenment or higher consciousness, aside from being useful in achieving physical and emotional health.

Chapter 2:
The Seven Chakras

Seven main chakras are present in the person's body. These chakras have great influence on one's mental, emotional and physical state. These chakras are also divided into three categories.

The Chakras of Matter

The first three chakras begin from the base of the spine and are present in the lower parts of the body. They are more physical in nature and govern mostly physical attributes and issues.

First Chakra: Root Chakra

The root chakra is also known as the base chakra. Its Sanskrit term is *Muladhara,* meaning "root support". It is the chakra of security and stability. It represents a person's basic needs, among which is the ability to feel grounded and secured. It encompasses the colon, bladder and the first three vertebrae. It is found at the base of the spine where the tailbone is.

Governed Body Areas:

- Spinal column

- Rectum

- Immune system

- Kidney

- Legs

Associated Physical Illnesses:

- Varicose veins
- Lower back pain
- Immunity disorders

Associated Emotional and Psychological Issues:

- Survival issues; money, food
- Self esteem

Second Chakra: Sacral Chakra

The second chakra is the Sacral chakra, also called *Svadhisthana* which translates into "one's own abode". The first syllable "Svad" has a meaning of its own that translates to "to taste with pleasure". It is depicted as having six vermillion petals similar to a lotus'.

This chakra holds the connection to one's desires, emotions and sexuality. It represents one's creativity and is responsible for one's ability to have balance and production. More in governance of sexuality, the sacral chakra brings balance between existing polarities such as spirit and matter, the feminine and the masculine, darkness and light, and self and others. It is found in the lower abdomen, two inches below the navel and another two inches in just above the pubic bone.

Governed Body Areas:

- Stomach
- Sexual Organs

- Upper intestine
- Gallbladder
- Pancreas

Associated Physical Illnesses:

- Lower Back Pain
- Pelvic Pain
- Urinary Illnesses

Emotional and Psychological Issues:

- Gender Issues
- Passion
- Productivity
- Sexuality
- Relationships
- Social

Third Chakra: Solar Plexus Chakra

The third chakra, *Manipura* translates to "lustrous gem". This chakra deals with personal power, which is one's ability to become confident in life and have control of it. It is found in the upper abdomen, at the stomach area from the navel to the breastbone. It is the source of personal power and governs one's self-worth, self-esteem and self-confidence. It governs a person's ego.

Governed Body Areas:

- Upper Abdomen
- Umbilicus to the Rib Cage
- Middle Spine
- Gallbladder
- Liver
- Kidney
- Stomach
- Small Intestine

Associated Physical Illnesses:

- Pancreatitis
- Indigestion
- Stomach Ulcers
- Anorexia or Bulimia
- Intestinal Tumors
- Cirrhosis
- Colon Diseases
- Hepatitis

Emotional and Psychological Issues:

- Fear of Rejection or Being Found Out
- Self Esteem Issues
- Oversensitivity to Criticism
- Indecisiveness

The Chakra Connecting Between Matter and Spirit

Only one chakra falls under this category, the middle chakra that is the heart chakra. It connects matter with spirit, the body with the soul.

Fourth Chakra: Heart Chakra

Anahata, the fourth chakra that means "unstruck" governs the heart and relates with the sense of being loved by others or oneself. The heart chakra is responsible for feelings of compassion, empathy, sympathy, and caring. It motivates a positive outlook towards other people such as understanding and forgiveness.

Governed Body Areas:

- Heart
- Rib Cage
- Blood
- Circulatory System
- Lungs

- Diaphragm
- Breasts
- Esophagus
- Thymus
- Shoulders
- Arms and Hands

Associated Physical Illnesses:

- Asthma
- Lung and Breast Cancer
- Pneumonia
- Thoracic Spine
- Upper Back and Shoulder Pain
- Heart Conditions

Emotional and Psychological Issues:

- Compassion
- Confidence
- Inspiration
- Generosity
- Hope

- Despair
- Envy
- Hate
- Jealousy
- Anger
- Fear

The Chakras of Spirit

The last three chakras relate with the spiritual experience and spiritual well-being. They are found from the throat up to the crown of the head. They are spiritual in nature and govern consciousness and mental and emotional issues.

Fifth Chakra: Throat Chakra

The fifth chakra is the *Vishuddha* chakra that translates to "especially pure". It is the center of one's will. The throat chakra is responsible for one's ability to express one's self honestly and completely, whether it is an opinion or emotion. This chakra deals with complete honesty.

Governed Body Areas:

- Throat
- Trachea
- Thyroid
- Esophagus

- Neck Vertebrae
- Mouth
- Teeth
- Gums

Associated Physical Illnesses:

- Sore Throat
- Laryngitis
- Voice Problems
- Mouth Ulcers
- Swollen Glands
- Thyroid Dysfunctions
- Gums and Teeth Problems

Emotional and Psychological Issues:

- Creativity
- Personal Expression
- Faith
- Addiction
- Criticism
- Decision Making

- Lack of Authority
- Will

Sixth Chakra: Eye/Third Eye Chakra

Ajna, the Sanskrit word for the sixth chakra means "command" and deals with insight. It refers to the mind center from which our avenue of wisdom comes from. With a healthy third eye chakra, one is able to separate reality from delusions and illusions. It separates small mindedness and helps develop impersonal but intuitive reasoning, therefore providing insight. The third eye chakra is located at the center of the forehead, just above the eyes.

Governed Body Areas:

- Neurological System and Brain
- Eyes, Ears, Nose
- Pituitary and Pineal Glands

Associated Physical Illnesses:

- Blindness
- Deafness
- Strokes
- Seizures
- Spinal Dysfunctions
- Brain Tumors

- Depression
- Learning Disabilities

Emotional and Physical Issues:

- Discipline
- Evaluation
- Wisdom
- Judgment
- Intuition
- Emotional Intelligence
- Fear of the Truth
- Confusion
- Concept of Reality

Seventh Chakra: Crown Chakra

The last chakra, the *Sahasrara,* is a Sanskrit word for "thousand", represented by the Lotus of a Thousand Petals. It is found on the top center of the head and deals with enlightenment and pure consciousness. The crown chakra also known as the light chakra is the tool that allows one to communicate with spiritual nature. It refers to the "God Source" of a person and is the key to becoming reconnected and one with the universe.

Governed Body Areas:

- Top Center of Head
- Midline Above Ears

Associated Physical Illnesses:

- Chronic Exhaustion not associated with Physical Ailments
- Sensitivity to Surroundings (Light, Environment, Sound)
- Diseases of the Skin, Muscular and Skeletal Systems
- Mystical Depression

Emotional and Psychological Issues:

- Discovery of the Divine
- Trust
- Humanitarianism
- Devotion
- Inspiration
- Values
- Selflessness
- Ethics
- Lack of Purpose
- Loss of Identity or Meaning in One's Life

Chapter 3:
Opening and Chakra Clearing

Energy flows through the body in the same way water flows through a river. It often passes through pools of water that circulate before flowing on to other pools. Each chakra is a pool of water from which the river of energy flows through. Ideally, these pools should be clean and the passages open so that the energy can flow freely. Life, however, is full of obstacles and certain events lead to the blocking of a chakra. Negative experiences are examples of what causes a blockage, as well as negative attitudes, thinking and habits.

Why you Should Open and Clear your Chakras

It is ideal for the chakras to be open because it allows balance in the body and mind. Indian tradition and beliefs suggest that in order to achieve a state of complete well-being, one must be in touch with their chakras, and have them opened and cleaned. Opening a chakra is done through reflection and the removal of negative factors that cause the blockage. In Yoga and Ayurvedic tradition, this is aided by certain breathing patterns, meditation and natural medicine. One can open the chakras through meditation alone, but with the help of a breathing pattern class and the guidance of a professional, the result can be intensely more effective.

Opening and Clearing the Chakras from Root to Crown

Each energy or chakra has a purpose as each represents an aspect of one's consciousness. In order to open the seven chakras, one must study each aspect represented and deal with the issues involved with it.

Opening the Root Chakra

The base chakra deals with survival and governs the feeling of being secure and safe. It is responsible for a person's sense of being grounded, or belonging to some place.

What Blocks the Chakra

The root chakra is blocked by fear - fear of the unknown and fear of insufficiency or being insufficient or unreliable. These fears include the troubles of everyday life such as financial stress, shelter and food worries. It also includes one's position in a society as a reliable person.

How to Open the Chakra

To be able to open the root chakra, learn to surrender the fears by not worrying about the far future; focus on the *now,* instead. Although financial stress is difficult to handle and issues regarding security and safety are hard to forget, learn to sit back and take a break. No matter what insufficiency the world or yourself is showing, it does not change the fact that all these are physical, replaceable and never lasting. Whatever trouble or doubt that lingers, accept that it will come to pass, along with the riches of the world that cannot be taken along with death.

Opening the Sacral Chakra

The second chakra deals with pleasure, sexuality, desires and passion. It governs over relationships including families, friends and lovers. It is influenced by life choices that are affected by and affect people involved in the situation. It governs all things that provide a person with happiness, in physical, emotional and mental terms.

<u>What Blocks the Chakra</u>

The sacral chakra revolves around physical and emotional pleasure and is blocked by guilt and self-blame. Making decisions are part of everyday life and certain choices gone wrong cause regret and ultimately self-blame.

<u>How to Open the Chakra</u>

What are the things that you blame yourself for? These thoughts and emotions prevent the flow of happiness in one's life. You must learn to forgive yourself for your transgressions and others' as well. Accept the reality that people make mistakes and you can't do anything to change the past. Meditate on what you can do to redeem yourself, but let go of what you cannot alter.

Opening the Solar Plexus Chakra

The third chakra deals with real power considered as self-power. It is responsible for one's confidence, ego and self-esteem.

<u>What Blocks the Chakra</u>

Shame blocks this chakra. People often have secrets about themselves or past experiences that they are ashamed of and prefer to hide away or forget. This becomes a burden, carried through time, and blocks the flow of self-empowerment. Self-disappointment reduces self-esteem and holds back potentiality.

<u>How to Open the Chakra</u>

You must be able to accept that you cannot deny certain aspects of your life, not even those parts of yourself that are disappointing. Accept the negative or unwanted part of yourself. Without these undesirable pasts, mistakes and qualities, you will not grow or become unique.

Opening the Heart Chakra

The fourth chakra deals with love - a love for all things, all people and one's self. It is responsible for feelings of care, sympathy, empathy and understanding. An open heart chakra encourages goodness in a person

<u>What Blocks the Chakra</u>

It is blocked by grief, loss and sadness. Understand that love is a form of energy and although people have experienced loss in different ways, like death, being left by loved ones or not loved back, there is always more of it being passed around.

<u>How to Open the Chakra</u>

To open the chakra of love, let the pain of loneliness flow away. Learn to feel love in all other things. Feel the love that nature provides - the warmth of the sun, the fruits of the trees and rainfall.

Opening the Throat Chakra

The fifth chakra, located at the throat, deals with pure truth. It is the validation of what is true and the acceptance of all things as they are. It is responsible for complete honesty in a person.

<u>What Blocks the Chakra</u>

It is blocked by lies. The throat chakra is often clogged when one tries to pretend to be someone else, or run away from his or her real passion. It is also blocked when you lie to others, about anything.

<u>How to Open the Chakra</u>

You cannot lie about your own nature and denying or trying to change what you truly want. Trying to escape what your heart loves will only prevent you from all you deserve and are capable of. Open the chakra by learning to accept who or what you really are.

Opening the 3rd Eye Chakra

This chakra deals with insight, and is blocked by illusion. The greatest illusion of the world is the illusion of separation. People believe and think that each person is different, but all is one and the same - connected.

<u>What Blocks the Chakra</u>

Discrimination, racism and maltreatment are some serious issues that people may experience with their sixth chakra blocked.

<u>How to Open the Chakra</u>

In order to open the light chakra for enlightenment, one must be able to treat others as equals. Although people, nations and beings are different in many ways, all are connected with each other and rely on each other's existence for a harmonious ecosystem that is the world.

Opening the Crown Chakra

The last chakra is referred to in meditation as the thought chakra. It deals with pure cosmic energy that is the highest level of awareness. It represents the full potential of a person by their connection to and being "one with the universe".

What Blocks the Chakra

It is blocked by earthly attachment ranging from love for a person, to value of physical or material possessions.

How to Open the Chakra

Meditate on what attaches you to the world; are you too attached? Do you value these destructible and temporary things too much? You cannot keep all these after life. Contemplate on what is more important, the person you love in physical form or the connection that grows and binds between you. Cherish these things, admire them if you may and give them complete value, and then let them go, forgotten. Surrender yourself completely, and only then will you come to realize what speck of dust we are and that life is hardly a second passing by.

Chapter 4:
Signs of Imbalance in your Chakras

It is possible to tell whether or not one's chakras are out of balance or need clearing. Below are the physical and emotional symptoms of imbalance in a particular chakra.

Imbalance in First Chakra

The root chakra is about self-preservation and belonging. The following are signs that one needs to clean or clear the root chakra:

<u>Physical Imbalances</u>

One can tell certain physical imbalances from a clogged root chakra. These problems are usually present in the legs, feet, tailbone, rectum and immune system. For males, problems in the reproductive organs and prostate gland could also occur. Most issues include degenerative arthritis, sciatica, constipation, knee or joint pain and eating disorders.

<u>Emotional & Psychological Imbalances</u>

When the first chakra is unbalanced, one feels the inability to provide the necessities in life such as food, shelter and money. There is a constant feeling of not having enough, of always having an impending shortage, debts and financial drought.

Imbalance in the Second Chakra

The second chakra located two inches below the navel is related with pleasure: one's ability to have fun, relax, be creative, be confident in their sexuality and experience true pleasure. This chakra allows us to relate with and enjoy the company of others.

Physical Imbalances

Since the sacral chakra is more attuned with sexual pleasure than most, physical issues caused by chakra imbalance include sexual and reproductive problems. Kidney dysfunctions, urinary problems and pain on the hip, lower back and pelvic area are other issues.

Emotional & Psychological Imbalances

A person may suffer emotional imbalance that has a drastic impact on their commitment to certain relationships. One becomes unable to express emotions or have fun and act based on desires. One also finds difficulty in determining their passions, or following them. There is fear of betrayal or impotence involved as well as the development of an addiction like alcoholism, smoking or binge eating.

Imbalance in the Third Chakra

The solar plexus chakra is located above the navel and helps us become aware of ourselves. It deals with how we view ourselves. It also rules over pride, confidence and egotism.

Physical Imbalances

Just above the navel, the solar plexus chakra governs over the stomach area and may cause stomach ulcers when imbalanced. Other physical imbalances also include issues with the gallbladder, pancreas and colon diseases. Liver dysfunction, high blood pressure, diabetes and chronic fatigue are also possible.

Emotional & Psychological Imbalances

Low self-esteem, issues with personal power and the emergence of the inner critic are results of imbalances in the solar plexus chakra. Fears of rejection may surface. One also becomes conscious of their physical appearance, or fears the criticism or simply the opinion of others.

Imbalance in the Fourth Chakra

The fourth chakra is the heart chakra and governs love in general.

Physical Imbalances

Heart diseases are impending issues involved in blocked heart chakras. Other physical imbalances include breathing issues like asthma, lung diseases and issues with the lymphatic system. Less critical issues are pain in the arm, wrists, upper back and shoulders. Women are also more prone to breast issues.

Emotional & Psychological Imbalances

Love is a freeing emotion and act, but if the heart chakra is blocked, closed or clogged, it can cause someone great difficulty when it comes to loving. These emotional imbalances include anger, jealousy and suffocation. One experiences feelings of abandonment, bitterness, envy and loneliness. One emotion that greatly affects a person is the inability to forgive.

Imbalance in the Fifth Chakra

The throat chakra helps you to express yourself freely and speak the truth.

Physical Imbalances

Physical imbalances include sore throats, problems around the neck like stiff neck, laryngitis and thyroid problems. Other facial problems may also be experienced like some pain on the cheek, chin, lips and tongue. Neck and shoulder pain can occur too.

Emotional & Psychological Imbalances

A balanced throat chakra enables a person to express themselves freely. With imbalance, one is unable to communicate well, both in written and spoken communication. There is a constant anxiety of having no power to make a difference and having no choice. This involves being unable to control what you mean and having little to no willpower when you need to defend yourself verbally.

Imbalance in the Sixth Chakra

The third eye chakra is at the center of the forehead, between the eyes. It refers to the invisible eye, which is supposed to allow one to see the bigger picture of things like situations, opportunities and the personalities of others.

Physical Imbalances

Unbalanced third eye chakra can be felt through physical issues like headaches, severe migraines and sinus issues. Other problems include blurriness in vision or deteriorating eyesight, eyestrain, loss of hearing and possibly loss of hormone functions.

Emotional & Psychological Imbalances

Emotional imbalances revolve around moodiness and can affect a person's self-reflection and volatility. There is a feeling of being unable to learn from others or see one's own fears. People suffering from an emotional imbalance from the sixth chakra tend to daydream a lot. They may even prefer the unreal world and have an exaggerated imagination. People who have completely blocked third eye chakras may be more prone to psychological issues, especially when other chakras are closed as well and they have no mutual support from others.

Imbalance in the Seventh Chakra

The crown chakra that provides a person with divine connection with the universe can cause great personal issues when at an imbalance.

Physical Imbalances

When the crown chakra is unbalanced or blocked, it is highly likely for a person to become depressed. It also triggers sensitivity to light, sound and the environment surface that brings about more physical issues and include most illnesses found from other chakras' imbalances.

Emotional & Psychological Imbalances

A person whose seventh chakra has become blocked or closed will have trouble finding his/her inner guidance or intuition. Spirituality and religion becomes a confusing aspect and one feels growing doubts about their beliefs. One becomes more and more prejudiced, close-minded and even unforgiving for fear of alienation or being wrong about themselves, their roots and beliefs.

Chapter 5:
Cleaning and Chakra Healing

Opened chakras are generally good for a person's well being. However, opening the chakras does not only allow positive energy, but also negative energy. Imagine a pool of water receiving the flow from a river. Water from the river is not always clean. Depending on the environment and ecosystem that the river comes from, the water it possesses may occasionally contain unclean substances.

The same can be said for chakras. Energy from the universe, other people, the environment and life experiences are not always pure and positive. When a person's chakras are open, they admit energy flow that is available to them, both positive and negative. With proper healing and clearing, it is possible to keep the chakras open and the flow of energy clean.

Why Chakras Need Cleaning and Healing

Sensitive people are prone to acquiring negative energies when their chakras are opened. It is because they are more aware of the energy they receive and are easily affected by its nature. This is an inevitable process, but affects people on different levels. Some may feel more troubled than others while some will be able to deal with and overcome issues.

Elements and Senses Relating to the Chakras

There are certain senses or elements related to every main chakra in the body. This association will help in healing an unbalanced or blocked chakra effectively.

Root Chakra – Sense of Smell, Earth Element

Sacral Chakra – Sense of Taste, Water Element

Solar Plexus Chakra – Sense of Sight, Fire Element

Heart Chakra – Sense of Touch, Air Element

Throat Chakra – Sense of Hearing, Element of Sound

Third Eye Chakra – The 6th Sense, Element of Light

Crown Chakra – Sense of Purity, Consciousness

Ideal Methods in Healing Each Chakra

In healing chakras, different methods are used for each one, as not all of them are the same in nature. The chakras located at the lower part of the body are more dense and associated more with the physical than those located at the upper part of the body.

Healing the Root Chakra

The first chakra is the densest chakra that relates the most to the physical body. To heal this chakra, physical activities like yoga and Pilates are ideal. Other methods include the use of smell-oriented therapy like aromatherapy coupled with body massage or stretching.

The use of gemstones as charms or decorations at home can help the flow of energy for the environment since gemstones come from the earth. By surrounding yourself with earthly elements like those mentioned above, you are brining sense of being at home or grounded with you wherever you go.

Healing the Sacral Chakra

Like the root, the sacral chakra is dense, but slightly less attuned with the physical body. It is still dense enough for physical methods such as Hatha Yoga, in particular. Hatha Yoga is a less intensive physical exercise. In fact, it is an introductory to Yoga and involves breathing exercises and stretch poses. Hatha Yoga will help improve one's posture, which can be associated with self-stability. This directly affects stability in relationships.

Eat healthy foods for sacral chakra healing. Since it is associated with the sense of taste; in reference to pleasure, sweet but healthy food like fruits will provide health and pleasure together.

Another physical activity to consider is Watson. This form of body therapy is done in warm water. The therapy includes breathing exercises, body massage, muscle stretching and sometimes meditation, all while submerged in warm water. The warmth and relaxing effect provides the sensuous pleasure that the sacral chakra aims to achieve.

Healing the Solar Plexus Chakra

Associated with the fire element, the solar plexus chakra can be healed through sunbathing. One does not necessarily have to get a tan. In fact, basking in the morning sun for 30 minutes to an hour will provide cleansing for the 3rd chakra.

People who feel particularly blocked from their solar plexus chakra, or are looking for a thorough cleansing, undergo fire-walking activities. It is a process where one must walk over a path of burning coals. It provides confidence in oneself when it comes to decision-making and courage in traversing the feared or unknown.

Healing the Heart Chakra

The heart chakra that governs love, in general, is motivated and healed through touch. Hugging is the ultimate method for healing the heart chakra. Ask your loved one to hug you or even hug yourself. The physical warmth provides a boost and balance in the heart energy.

Breathing techniques work well because the heart chakra is influenced by the air element. It helps to level one's breathing which allows the circulation of blood through the body to flow freely, and therefore provide the heart and other organs with energy.

EFT or Emotional Freedom Technique is a form of therapy involving acupressure. It aims to level one's emotions through certain pressure points in the body, most of which are located on the upper portion. This will allow a person's mood to have balance.

Healing the Throat Chakra

The throat chakra is surprisingly associated with and influenced by the element of sound and the sense of hearing. It is important that one should be able to listen first, before expressing themselves. This helps in avoiding miscommunication.

To heal the throat chakra and the inability to express truthfully, invest in mediation focused on sound. One technique for sound healing is to create the sounds personally, through either meditative sounds or singing. Let nothing but the sound flow through your vocal chords and focus on nothing but that. Another way to perform sound healing is to use crystals or glass for creating such sounds. The sound is purer this way and the act of listening is practiced.

The health of the throat chakra depends on how honest one expresses himself or herself. The challenge lies in expressing oneself truthfully despite the difficult situations that make lying seem more ideal. Practice honesty and avoid lying because it violates the body and the spirit.

Healing the 6th Sense Chakra

Meditation is the best method for cleaning and healing a blocked 6th sense chakra. Because it deals with pure truth, the 6th sense chakra can be cleansed through visualization. Because the 3rd eye is not physical, rely on your intuition. Meditate to find whatever answer or solution necessary in overcoming personal or worldly issues that are clogging the 6th chakra.

Healing the Crown Chakra

Related with pure consciousness, self-reflection and meditation help in healing and maintaining the crown chakra. Focus on pure and thoughtless openness, not just open-mindedness. While meditating, aim to achieve an openness that stretches beyond the self and others. Open your mind, heart, awareness and soul to the world itself with all life included. This will allow pure consciousness without the distraction of earthly attachments.

Chapter 6:
Chakra Meditation

Meditation is the practice of self-reflection and turning your attention to one point of reference. It is a practice done by monks and influenced modern people, which greatly helps in natural healing, and emotional and physical well-being. Chakra meditation is performed in order to open the chakras, as well as provide it balance and healing. Meditation is an important practice in maintaining the passageway of every chakra.

Chakra meditation is an excellent way to recharge and improve energy flow. Life's obstacles and uncontrollable situations often lead people to lose their confidence, self-awareness, love for others, and so on. Meditating will help return positivity into one's life, a calmer demeanor and the ability to focus and see life at its best and in a bigger picture.

How to Begin Chakra Meditation

Find a place where you can stay in for 30 minutes without any disturbance. It is preferable to have no phone along with you or at least set it on silent mode.

Set or Find an Ideal Environment

Bring a mat or rug and spread it out on the floor. If you can meditate on a chair, sitting undisturbed with a straight posture will suffice. It is preferable to sit on the floor with legs crossed. This helps you become rooted or feel in touch with the earth more. Make sure your children or pets are elsewhere.

The purpose is to eliminate distractions so you can focus on your meditation. If possible, ask a relative, your spouse or a guardian to take care of your children or pets in the meantime. The meditation process is only half an hour after all. Meditating early in the morning is an ideal time, it will be quiet while others are still sleeping or just beginning the day.

Meditation Tips and Preparation

If you are having trouble imagining or focusing on a chakra, do not be disheartened. This simply means that this certain chakra is unbalanced and will require more attention and time.

Be prepared for your meditation. Sign up for a chakra meditation class or ask a guide so that you can do it properly and in the correct way. If you prefer, search online for video guides on where to begin and how to deal with each chakra imbalance. You will be able to do it on your own after a few sessions of chakra meditation.

Chakra meditation takes 30 minutes. Each chakra should have at least three to four minutes of meditation.

How to Meditate Effectively

Use your imagination when meditating. The chakras are not physical in nature so one cannot focus on them visually. Instead, imagine a presence or the energy where the chakra focused on is located. If you are meditating on your crown chakra, then focus on the energy that resides on the top of your head. Imagine a flow of energy over your head and this will usually result in the feeling of something lingering overhead.

In chakra meditation, imagining a white light as the flowing energy of balance and healing is the center of attention.

The meditation begins in imagining the light on the crown of the head, moving down towards the root chakra. This practice is associated with receiving positive energy from the universe down towards and throughout the body. The meditation for energy balance begins at the top to let it evenly flow down to the rest of the chakras.

Remember that in chakra meditation, the idea is to become open to accept energy from the universe and allow it to flow through the body and achieve balanced chakras.

Chapter 7:
The History of Chakras

The history of Chakras will have you going back to the beginning of time. It is said that the real birthplace of the human race is in Tanzania, and a certain Mount Meru, also known as a mystical mountain is located here.

Mount Meru is believed to be where the Goddess Shri Lalita, who was the main source of the nine interlocking triangles—or chakras—used to reside. She represents the union of the masculine and feminine, and also symbolizes the intersection of power from different parts of the body.

Mount Meru also signifies one's journey from the start or bottom of their life, all the way to the top, which shows where chakras and the energy system began.

Indian Tradition

The thing about Mount Meru is that it also appears in both Indian and Egyptian Mythology, which coincides with the Vedas, known as the oldest written Indian traditions. These date back to 1,500 to 500 B.C.

The Vedas are recorded from the Brahmins Caste. They entered India from the North and propagated Aryan stock as a means of gratitude to Shri Lalita. The term "Chakra" was then born.

The Birth of Chakras

Originally, chakra denoted the meaning of "wheels", which symbolized *cakravartin*s, or the chariot wheels of rulers. It was also used as a metaphor for the sun.

Ancient Hindus believed that the sun could traverse the world like the most triumphant and skilled chariot. It also represents balance and eternal order, more than anything in the world.

With the birth of chakras came the dawn of a new age. This signified the emergence of Vishnu, one of the three main deities of Hinduism. Vishnu is often referred to as the *Protector* or the *Preserver*.

Vishnu is said to have descended from the earth, holding a conch shell, a lotus flower, a cakra, and a club in his four arms. A cakra is a weapon that resembles a discus.

Psychic Centers of Consciousness

The Upanishads then began teachings of chakras that are still being used and adhered to up to today. This started in 600 BC, and the teachings were adapted by the Yoga Sutras of Patanjali in 200 BC.

Chakras in Patanjali were said to interpret:

1. Pure Consciousness (Purusha)

2. Prima Materia of the World (Prakriti)

They believed that by doing yoga, one could awaken their chakras, and rise above 'plain' consciousness in order to realize 'pure' consciousness. This way, the mind would not fluctuate because of emotions, especially anger and loneliness. This would also invoke a higher, and much deeper kind of synthesis.

The Rise of the Chakra System and Kundalini Yoga

The Tantric Tradition then gave way to the rise of the chakra system, with the help of Kundalini Yoga. This happened in the Common Era, also known as the second half of the first millennium.

Tantra literally means "tool for stretching", which made people believe that by doing yoga exercises, they'd be able to tap into their chakras. However, it all started as a sexual tradition, but over the years, these practices were also used to give recognition to deities and goddesses. By doing so, one is believed to be able to integrate the universe's many polaric forces.

The 1900s

In 1919, the first manuscript that's believed to explain chakras was introduced to the West by a man named Arthur Avalon. This book was entitled *The Serpent Power*.

In the said book, he was able to explain various practices that people did—and can do—to awaken the chakras, including the ways one has to meditate in order to tap into various chakras. This is called *Gorakshashatakam*, which is now deemed as the precursor of today's Chakra theory, together with Tantric Sex, and Kundalini Yoga.

The Seven Chakras

With the help of *Gorakshashatakam*, the seven basic chakras that inhibit the subtle body were named. These now correspond to nerve ganglias in the spinal column. These are:

1. **Root Chakra.** This represents the feeling of being grounded, and is deemed to be the foundation of all

chakras. It is located at the tailbone area of the spine, and is related to issues of survival (hunger, financial, etc.).

2. **Sacral Chakra.** Next is the Sacral Chakra which is located in the lower abdomen and denotes one's ability to experience adventures and connect with others. It is also related to a sense of pleasure, well-being, abundance, and sexuality.

3. **Solar Plexus Chakra.** Located in the upper abdomen, this denotes a person's ability to be in control of their life, and to be confident, as well. It also deals with issues of self-esteem and self-worth.

4. **Heart Chakra.** As the name suggests, this has a lot to do with a person's ability to love, and is located just above the heart, in the center of one's chest. It deals with joy, peace, love, and healing.

5. **Throat Chakra.** Located in the throat, this denotes one's ability to communicate, and is also related to the truth and feelings of self-expression.

6. **Third Eye Chakra.** This denotes one's ability to focus and see the bigger picture, and is located between the eyes in the forehead. It is also related to one's ability to think, wisdom, and intuition.

7. **Crown Chakra.** Finally, there is the crown chakra which is also known as the highest chakra of all. This is located on top of the head and is also related to one's connection with his spirituality, together with inner and outer beauty.

Chapter 8:
Why Your Chakras May Be Imbalanced or Blocked

There are times when your chakras may be blocked or imbalanced. This often happens because of emotional upset, caused by either accidents, conflicts, or any form of loss.

There are also times when you get overly stressed and anxious and in turn, your chakras suffer. When this happens, harmony is lost and one may suffer from certain diseases or problems.

Here are some of the problems that could lead to a blockage of the chakras.

Root Chakra

The Root Chakra suffers when you feel like you cannot protect or cover your basic needs, or when you feel like you cannot put your necessities in order. When this happens, your prostate may be affected if you're a man, and you could experience problems with your feet, legs, reproductive organs, and immune system. This can also then lead to eating disorders, sciatica, knee pain, and even degenerative arthritis.

To get this back in balance, you have to start believing that you have the right to be on earth and that you have an important role to play.

Once you get this back in balance, you'll feel grounded, supported, and connected to the world.

Sacral Chakra

The Sacral Chakra is affected when you cannot express your emotions well, and when you cannot stay committed. It is affected when you fear things too much, when you give in to your addictions, and when you betray yourself and the people around you.

This then causes urinary problems, sexual and reproductive issues, low back and pelvic pain.

In order to get this back in balance, you should allow yourself to take risks, stay committed, and stay creative. You also have to learn to be passionate, outgoing, and positively sexual.

Solar Plexus Chakra

When your self-esteem is low and when you feel like you cannot believe in yourself, your Solar Plexus Chakra suffers. It also suffers when you fear criticism because of being criticized too much in the past, or when you don't feel good about your physical appearance.

When that happens, you might experience digestive problems, high blood pressure, liver dysfunction, and problems in the colon and intestines.

In order to get this back in balance, you have to make sure that you accept yourself—no matter who or what you are; or what you can and cannot do. When that happens, you'll be able to have more self-respect and compassion, and you will be more confident and assertive.

Heart Chakra

When you love people to the point of suffocation, your heart chakra suffers. It also suffers when you become overly jealous, bitter, angry, or when you abandon others without notice. This then leads to heart diseases, asthma, lymphatic system problems, breast cancer, shoulder and upper arm problems, as well as wrist pain.

You can get the heart chakra back in balance by always letting joy, compassion, and gratitude rule over your life. You should also learn to let forgiveness flow and learn to give trust, as well.

When that happens, you'll learn how to love—whether yourself, or also the people around you.

Throat Chakra

The Throat Chakra gets to be blocked when you cannot speak or write about your thoughts clearly, and when you feel like others are dictating what you have to do for you. In short, you'd get to feel as if you do not have any choices at all. This can lead to a sore throat, thyroid issues, facial problems, ulcers, and ear infections, together with neck and shoulder pain.

In order to get this back in order, you have to make sure that you let your voice be heard and that you speak your mind. When this happens, you'll be able to be honest and firm, expressive, communicative, and also be a good listener.

Third Eye Chakra

The Third Eye Chakra is said to be the most complicated, and certainly not the easiest one to open. When you get too moody or let your emotions cloud your judgment, this chakra is affected. This is also affected when you daydream too much and let your imagination burn reality down. More than that, it is blocked when you forget to reflect on the state of your life, and when you become volatile—in whichever way possible.

In order to stop the blockage, you should learn to look at the big picture instead of overanalyzing things. Once this happens, you'll be able to have some clarity; you'll be able to focus on things that need your attention, be able to recognize fears and not let them take over your life, and get to learn from others, as well.

Crown Chakra

Finally, you have to understand your crown chakra. This gets blocked when you're always trying to find greater power than you have, and when you have problems using your knowledge and skills for the best. Sometimes, it also gets affected when you let political and religious problems bother you too much, when you carry prejudices against others, when you over-analyze, and when you are scared of being alienated or being alone.

In order to stop this from being blocked, you should aim to live mindfully and have clarity of mind. When this is achieved, you'll easily be able to live in the moment and have the kind of wisdom and inner guidance that's unshakable and true.

Chapter 9:
Affirmations for Improving Your Chakras

Aside from the given guidelines earlier, it's also important to take note that you can also make use of affirmations to heal and improve the state of your chakras.

Read on and find out about the affirmations you could utter for each chakra!

Root Chakra

The biggest challenge for the root chakra is fear—so you need to develop courage, and realize that you're meant for bigger and better things. For that, you could use these affirmations below:

1. I am a peaceful, divine being of light.

2. I am protected. I am peaceful, and secure.

3. I am connected to my body; I am deeply rooted.

4. Just like a star or a tree, I feel safe and secure.

5. I have a right to be here on earth; my presence certainly means something.

6. I stand for justice, and truth; I stand for my values.

7. I can stand on my own two feet; I am grounded and stable.

8. I am grateful for the challenges in my life; I have the capacity to overcome them.

9. I trust myself, and make choices that are healthy for me.

10. I trust in the goodness of life; I trust that the choices I make will help me grow and transform.

11. I love my life, and I trust myself.

Sacral Chakra

Being your body's passion and pleasure center, the main challenge here would be guilt, which can be combated by taking risks and also by believing in yourself. Here are the chakra affirmations that you should utter:

1. I enjoy my body; I love my body.

2. I have healthy boundaries; I know how to take care of myself, and of my body.

3. I am open to using my senses in order to experience and appreciate the present moment.

4. I am appreciative of every breath I take; I have a lot of pleasure in my life.

5. I value and respect my body.

6. I am allowing myself to experience pleasure.

7. I am open to touch, and to be touched.

8. Emotions are the language of my soul.

9. I know that my sexuality is sacred; I vow to take care of it.

10. I am at peace; I can take care of my physical body.

Solar Plexus Chakra

The main challenge that the Solar Plexus Chakra faces is how you can be aware of your personal power, and how you'll be able to use it in a way that's balanced and fair. In short, you have to be responsibly conscious, and you have to be able to react to the circumstances in your life in the right way.

Here are affirmations that you could use:

1. I love and accept myself.
2. I am strong and courageous; I can stand up for myself.
3. I know how to choose the best for myself.
4. I am worthy of respect, kindness, and love.
5. I am proud of all my achievements; I know I did my best to deserve them.
6. I feel my own power.
7. I direct my own life.
8. I am authentic.
9. I honor myself.
10. I am at peace with myself.
11. I seek opportunities not only for personal, but also for spiritual growth.
12. I am free to choose in any situation.

Heart Chakra

The Heart Chakra is able to move you through your life. It's able to help you get in touch with yourself and appreciate life more—and that's why its biggest challenge is grief. You can use the following affirmations to improve this chakra:

1. I am open to love.
2. I accept myself completely and deeply because all love resides in my heart.
3. I am wanted; I am loved.
4. I nurture my inner child; I believe he/she is still and always will be important in my life.
5. I can forgive myself, and I always will.
6. I love and appreciate animals; I love and appreciate the natural world.
7. I accept things as they are.
8. I am one with the animals, and one with nature; I feel a sense of unity with the world.
9. I am connected to other human beings.
10. I am grateful for all the challenges in my life.
11. I am open to kindness; I am always open to life.

Throat Chakra

The Throat Chakra is one of the most spiritual chakras. This inspires you to be creative and expressive—as well as being honest with yourself. Its main challenge are lies—you have to be able to see through them, and at the same time, make sure that lies do not rule your life.

Here are the affirmations you could utter:

1. I am honest in my communication; I am open, and I am clear.
2. I can communicate my feelings with ease.
3. I have a right to speak my truth.
4. I can resolve my life's challenges through strong will.
5. I can express myself through art, writing, and speech.
6. I have integrity.
7. I live an authentic life.
8. I nourish my spirit through creativity.
9. I am at peace.
10. I take good care of my body.
11. I realize my truth by listening to what my mind and body says.
12. I express gratitude towards my life.
13. I know when it's time to listen; I do not deny it.

Third-Eye Chakra

The Third Eye Chakra is also spiritual in the sense that it allows you to appreciate both your inner and outer worlds.

Your main challenge here is illusion. You have to know how to blur the lines between reality and fiction; you have to learn to live in the real world, while still being able to use your imagination.

Here are affirmations you could try:

1. I am the source of my truth; I am the source of love.
2. I am at peace.
3. My life is able to move effortlessly.
4. I am open to inspiration; I am open to bliss.
5. I am connected with the universe's wisdom.
6. I know that all is well in my world.
7. I love and accept myself.
8. I forgive myself.
9. I forgive the past; I make use of its lessons as guiding stones in life.
10. I trust my intuition.
11. I listen to the wisdom of my elders.
12. I nurture my spirit.
13. I am intuitive and wise, and connected with my inner guide.
14. I try to understand and learn from my experiences.
15. I listen to my deepest wisdom.

16. I am in touch with my inner guidance.

Crown Chakra

Finally, you have the crown chakra, which helps you become selfless and unite with every part of your body. Its biggest challenge is attachment. You have to see everything as a passing thing—as everything in life will come and go eventually.

This way, it will be easy for you to accept change—and understand that it's really the only constant thing in life. Here are some affirmations you could use:

1. I am at peace.
2. My life moves with grace.
3. I am open to divine wisdom.
4. I am connected with the universe's wisdom.
5. I know that all is well in my world.
6. I accept and love myself.
7. I am grateful for all the goodness in my life.
8. I live in the present moment.
9. I am open to letting go of my attachments.
10. I trust my intuition.
11. I listen to the wisdom of the universe.
12. I seek experiences that I know will nourish my spirit.

13. I cherish my spirit.

14. I seek to understand and learn from the experiences I've had in life.

15. I honor the Divine within me.

16. I am part of the Divine.

By using these affirmations, you'll be able to improve the state of your chakras—and experience a life that's full of love and peace.

Chapter 10:
How Yoga Can Help Your Chakras

According to Tantric Yogis, yoga is able to help you improve your chakras. Yoga has been used for thousands of years to help in opening the chakras and getting in touch with them.

You see, yogis believe that chakras resemble spinning wheels, because they involve a convergence of thoughts, feelings, and energy, together with their physical bodies. When this happens, you'll be able to separate reality from your emotions, be able to separate confidence from fear, and separate desires from aversions. When you practice yoga, you'll learn to unravel any blocks that may hinder you from tapping into your highest potential.

Here's how yoga can help each of your chakras.

Root Chakra

The center of this chakra is found at the pelvic floor. It makes you connected to the earth as it is the root of your soul. It keeps you secure and physically strong, helps you stay in touch with reality, and bring awareness to your center.

As it is the realm of fears and avoidance, you'd understand how your urges will revolve around food, sex, sleep, and survival. It also holds your most latent potential. This means that when you do yoga, you'll be able to breathe life into the root's sleeping power. The best poses for this include the Chair Pose, Warrior Pose, hip openers, squats, and lunges.

Sacral Chakra

Meanwhile, your Sacral Chakra is your water center. This is not only the home of your reproductive organs—it is also the home of your desire. It's important to take care of this chakra because if not, your life may be ruled by attachments—and that is often unhealthy.

Once you do yoga, you'll learn to let your consciousness move freely and with that you'll be able to access your potential to make way for sensual pleasure and healing.

For this chakra, you could try deep lunges, asanas, forwards lunges, hip openers, and the Chair Pose, as well.

Solar Plexus Chakra

Next, you have the Solar Plexus Chakra. This is often associated with individual power and purpose, as well as one's passion and fire. This holds a vast amount of your vitality. When this chakra is blocked, you might have problems with your ambition and with gaining physical power.

The most recommended pose for this are the yoga twists.

Heart Chakra

In Himalayan Tradition, this chakra is believed to be the most powerful of all. Some even consider it to be the very seat of one's soul. This is the meeting ground of all emotional experience.

Yoga can allow your heart chakra to radiate the highest aspects of being a person, which includes compassion, total faith in the Divine, and finally, unconditional love. This will also help you deal with your deepest insecurities, loneliness, and disappointment.

In order to open this up, you can make use of backbends and *pranayama* meditation.

Throat Chakra

As the throat chakra is associated with the element of ether, this helps control your metabolism. It is the home of hearing and speech.

With the help of yoga, you'll be able to tap into your spiritual self—and make sure that you develop a better relationship with the Divine.

The best exercises for this are Asanas, the Fish Pose, the Shoulder Stand, the Camel, and the Plow.

Third Eye Chakra

Being the command center of the chakras, this is important in regularizing the energy streams in your body, especially where the mind and body converge. It is connected to your development and growth because it works directly on the pituitary gland.

With the help of yoga, you'll achieve relaxed consciousness, and also be able to improve your intuition; you'd understand that you are more than just a physical body—and that you have an important place in this world.

The best practices here are the Chair, and central breathing exercises.

Crown Chakra

And of course, there is the Crown Chakra. Almost any kind of yoga pose works great for this, and with their help, you'll be able to let go of your individual ego, understand your personal and linear needs, and also be able to process your emotional experiences.

Chapter 11:
How Crystals Can Help Your Chakras

Finally, you should never neglect crystals. In fact, they're an important part of chakra healing. When crystals are placed directly over your chakras, they're able to give off divine healing energy that is released through the energy channels in your body. This then makes its way to the aura and changes it for the better. You can use crystals by placing them directly over your chakras for a period of time, carrying them on you, or having them placed around the home. Having them make contact with your skin is best, particularly if over their corresponding chakra. Many people like to wear them on a bracelet or necklace.

Root Chakra: Garnet

Garnet is deemed as the crystal of the Root Chakra. It's the color red, and works with the Root Chakra because it's able to keep you inspired and grounded. It helps you become motivated to achieve your goals in life, and to make sure that you do your best, no matter happens.

With the help of Garnet, you'll be connected to the earth—you'll be able to fight addictions, material desires, and being attached to material things—because life is so much more than that.

Sacral Chakra: Carnelian

Next, you have Carnelian, which is known as the best crystal for the Sacral Chakra. It gives you a better understanding of humans, and human life, as a whole. More than that, it's also able to help hone your creativity, give you emotional balance, and help you have unity with yourself and with the people around you.

Use Carnelian if you're having problems in these areas.

Solar Plexus Chakra: Citrine

The Solar Plexus Chakra is responsible for your connection with the astral world—and even with your own astral body. When it's out of balance, you might be hypersensitive and overly emotional.

With the help of Citrine, you will be able to neutralize the negative energies that you have in your life. You'd be able to protect yourself, and normalize mood swings so that you can be more appreciative of what's going on in your life. More than that, you'd also be able to let abundance and success be in your mindset, so you'll be motivated to do your best to achieve what you want. It will end your depression and self-doubt—and help you become a much happier individual!

Heart Chakra: Aventurine

Green Aventurine is the best crystal for the heart chakra. It's always good to take care of the heart chakra because it's quite sensitive. When not given enough attention, it may cause you to feel separate from others. It also prevents you from loving people unconditionally.

However, with the help of Aventurine, you can put things back in order. You'll be able to set realistic goals, and remind yourself to do your best in order for them to be achieved. It calms you down, and prevents you from being angry or irritated at times when you have to remain composed. It heals circulation and helps you be more in touch with yourself, balancing male-female energy in the process. It also promotes compassion and empathy; it makes you understand you're not the only important person on earth; others matter, too.

Throat Chakra: Jolite

Jolite works with the throat chakra's main color of blue. It's a crystal that makes way for clear expression, and also keeps the lines of communication open. When it works with the chakra, it's able to help you figure out what's right for you, and tell you what you should feel inside.

Jolite is able to help you speak from the mind and from the heart—and not just one of them at a time. It's able to help you speak your truth so that everything in your life can easily flow, and as a result you'll be able to manifest positivity in any part of your life. Jolite is also able to promote leadership, power, self-confidence, and inner strength—helping you express yourself way better than before!

Third Eye Chakra: Amethyst

Not only is amethyst one of the most popular stones out there, it's also essential for the improvement of the third eye chakra. You see, when the third eye chakra is out of balance, you'll find it hard to meditate and attach yourself with your inner being. You might also have an irrational and intense fear of death, and may also be depressed.

As Amethyst is known as the stone of meditation, it has natural calming and healing qualities. It's able to bring harmony, peace, and calmness into your life. It also develops intuition, increases your attention, and helps you to train your mind to make lucid dreaming possible. Aside from that, it gets rid of compulsive behaviors—and always makes you feel at peace with yourself, with the world, and all the other beings in it.

Crown Chakra: Rainbow Moonstone

And lastly, you have rainbow moonstone for the crown chakra. The colors pink, purple, and white are predominant in the crown chakra, so it's fitting that a colorful crystal is also used for it.

As the name suggests, people believe that the rainbow moonstone has some connections to the moon and that it has quite some magic of its own. The said magic allows you to open up your heart and mind to spiritual development, and helps you appreciate spiritual experiences. It helps you forget the illusion of time, and allows you to be calm while making use of ancient wisdom to rule over your life.

Conclusion

Thank you again for downloading this book!

I hope this book was able to help you learn more about chakras!

The next step is to put this information to use, and begin focusing on your chakras to improve your health and wellbeing!

Also don't forget to download my **FREE** report on the 7 Keys for Successful Meditation by following the link - http://bit.ly/1F91lfl

Finally, if you enjoyed this book, please take the time to share your thoughts and post a review on Amazon. It'd be greatly appreciated!

Thank you and good luck!

www.ingramcontent.com/pod-product-compliance
Lightning Source LLC
LaVergne TN
LVHW021736060526
838200LV00052B/3315